Daily Journal

Daily Journal

Daily Journal

Daily Journal

Daily Journal

Daily Journal

Daily Journal

Daily Journal

Daily Journal

Daily Journal

Daily Journal

Daily Journal

Daily Journal

Daily Journal

Daily Journal

Daily Journal

Daily Journal

Daily Journal

Daily Journal

Daily Journal

Daily Journal

Daily Journal

Daily Journal

Daily Journal

Daily Journal

Daily Journal

Daily Journal

Daily Journal

Daily Journal

Daily Journal

Daily Journal

Daily Journal

Daily Journal

Daily Journal

Daily Journal

Daily Journal

Daily Journal

Daily Journal

Daily Journal

Daily Journal

Daily Journal

Daily Journal

Daily Journal

Daily Journal

Daily Journal

Daily Journal

Daily Journal

Daily Journal

Daily Journal

Daily Journal

Daily Journal

Daily Journal

Daily Journal

Daily Journal

Daily Journal

Daily Journal

Daily Journal

Daily Journal

Daily Journal

Daily Journal

Daily Journal

Daily Journal

Daily Journal

Daily Journal

Daily Journal

Daily Journal

Daily Journal

Daily Journal

Daily Journal

Daily Journal

Daily Journal

Daily Journal